FINDING YOUR BLUEPRINT

By Gary Madlock

© Copyright 2022 by Gary Madlock

All rights reserved. No part of this publication may be reproduced, stored in a retrieval system, or transmitted in any form or by any means—electronic, mechanical, photocopy, recording, or any other—except for brief quotations in printed reviews, without the express written permission from the author. Reach him at: www.findingyourblueprint.org

Scripture quotations marke (AMP) are taken from the Amplified® Bible (AMP), Copyright © 2015 by The Lockman Foundation. Used by permission. www.lockman.org

Scripture quotations marked (KJV) are taken from the King James Version of the Holy Bible, which is in the public domain.

Scripture quotations marked (NKJV) are taken from the New King James Version®. Copyright © 1982 by Thomas Nelson. Used by permission. All rights reserved.

Scripture quotations marked MSG are taken from THE MESSAGE, copyright © 1993, 2002, 2018 by Eugene H. Peterson. Used by permission of NavPress. All rights reserved. Represented by Tyndale House Publishers, Inc.

Cover Photo: istockphoto.com/1035342734/Michael Burrell

ISBN: 9798849646879

Table of Contents

Introduction	5
Chapter One: The Original Blueprint	7
Chapter Two: Missing Your Blueprint	13
Chapter Three: Connecting With Your Blueprint	19
Chapter Four: Building Your Infrastructure	27
Chapter Five: What You Are Worth	39
Chapter Six: What You Have	47
Chapter Seven: Why You Are Here	59
Closing Thoughts	73

Introduction

Did you know that God knew you before you were born? Whether you got here through a planned or an unplanned pregnancy, God already knew you, wanted you, and had a purpose for you.

God's purpose for your life contains a divinely drawn blueprint, in which He defines five things: 1) what you are, 2) who you are, 3) what you are worth, 4) what you have, and 5) why you are here. You are not an accident or a mistake. You belong on this earth for a reason. From the day you were born, you have had an inherent desire to find your blueprint, and you've been searching for it all your life.

As you study the pages of this book, you're going to see what you've never seen, go where you've never been, do what you've never done, and have what you've never had. 1 Corinthians 2:9-10 says:

"But as it is written, Eye has not seen, nor ear heard, neither have entered into the heart of man, the things which God hath prepared for them that love him. But God has revealed them unto us by his Spirit: for the Spirit searches all things, yea, the deep things so God." (KJV)

Right now, God is saying to you, "I'm inviting you to come on a journey with Me to discover the things I have prepared for you that you've never heard about or seen before. As you walk with Me, I'm going to introduce you to the person I created you to be. Once you see yourself the way I designed you to be, you'll begin to function the way I created you to live. As you live according to My design, you'll do what I created you to do on earth. This is where you'll finally find that lasting fulfillment, satisfaction, and contentment you've been looking for all your life.

Then you'll understand the words I spoke in John 10:10: where the thief comes only in order to steal, kill and destroy. I came that you might have and enjoy life, and have it in abundance (to the full, till it overflows)." (AMP)

Let's begin this journey!

Chapter One
The Original Blueprint

A blueprint is a plan or drawing that shows the look and function of something before it is built. These drawings define all the construction specifications. Before you were born, God drew a blueprint for your life, which defined five things: 1) what you are, 2) who you are, 3) what you are worth, 4) what you have, and 5) why you are here.

We can see what this looks like in the life of Jeremiah. God told Jeremiah in chapter 1, verse 5:

> "Before I formed you in the womb I knew and approved of you (as My chosen instrument), and before you were born I separated and set you apart, consecrating you; and I appointed you as a prophet to the nations." (AMP)

We can also see what this looks like in the life of the Apostle Paul. Galatians 1:15-16 says:

"But when God, who had chosen me and set me apart before I was born, and called me through His grace, was pleased to reveal His Son in me so that I might preach Him among the Gentiles [as the good news—the way of salvation], I did not immediately consult with anyone [for guidance regarding God's call and His revelation to me]." (AMP)

In Ephesians 1:4-5 we see the original plan for who God wanted us to be:

"just as [in His love] He chose us in Christ [actually selected us for Himself as His own] before the foundation of the world, so that we would be holy [that is, consecrated, set apart for Him, purpose-driven] and blameless in His sight. In love He predestined and lovingly planned for us to be adopted to Himself as [His own] children through Jesus Christ, in accordance with the kind intention and good pleasure of His will." (AMP)

In addition, Jeremiah 29:11 says:

> "For I know the thoughts and plans I have for you, says the Lord, thoughts and plans for welfare and peace and not for evil, to give you hope in your final outcome." (AMP)

How does it make you feel knowing God specifically planned for you to be on earth? Just pause a moment and imagine God drawing a blueprint for your life.

In a world filled with millions of people, we can have a difficult time imagining God caring for us as individuals. Many people say, "God has too many other things that are more important to deal with than to worry about me." This could not be further from the truth. Psalm 139:13-18 says:

> "For You did form my inward parts; You did knit me together in my mother's womb. I will confess and praise You for you are fearful and wonderful and for the awful wonder of my birth! Wonderful are Your works, and that my inner self knows right well. My frame was not hidden from You when I was being formed in secret and intricately and curiously wrought (as if embroidered

with various colors) in the depths of the earth (a region of darkness and mystery). Your eyes saw my unformed substance, and in Your book all the days of my life were written before ever they took shape, when as yet there were none of them. How precious and weighty also are Your thoughts to me, O God! How vast is the sum of them! If I could count them, they would be more in number than the sand. When I awoke, (could I count to the end) I would still be with You." (AMP)

God didn't just throw you together. He designed you for a purpose. You are awesomely and respectfully made in the eyes of God. He is still waiting on so many people to see themselves the way He designed them to be. This is why He wants you to find your blueprint.

God drew your blueprint to give you a vision. Before someone builds a house, the builder gets an architectural drawing of what the house will look like. Then a set of blueprints are drawn up with all the specifications detailing exactly how the house will be built. Then the plans are presented to a contractor.

The contractor then gets the materials to put the house together. As he builds the house according to the blueprint, the image on the plans becomes the real physical house. Similarly, when you operate according to your original blueprint, the image of what God says you are, who you are, what you are worth, what you have, and why you are here will become a reality.

If the contractor doesn't follow the plans for the house, it will not look or function the way it was designed. The toilet could end up in the middle of the living room, the shower could end up in the laundry room, or the kitchen sink could end up in the corner of the master bedroom.

If you don't build according to the blueprint, you will end up with a life that never looks the way God designed it too look or function the way He designed it to work. As a result, you will end up feeling confused, frustrated, disappointed, dissatisfied, and depressed. Proverbs 29:18 says, "Where there is no vision the people perish:" (KJV) And Psalm 127:1 says, "Except the Lord build the house, they labor in vain, that build it;". (KJV) Imagine getting to the end of your life only to discover all your labor has been in vain.

Many individuals who have all the things money can buy have still said to their close friends, "I don't know what it is, but something is missing." How do we miss our blueprint?

Chapter Two
Missing Your Blueprint

One morning while I was in prayer, scriptures about God knowing us before we were born and His plan for our lives kept popping up inside me. As I was meditating on these scriptures, thinking about a plan, I began to see a blueprint. Immediately I knew God was showing me something. I heard Him say, "Go to Romans 3:23." As I was reading it, the Lord stopped me after I'd read the first part, "For all have sinned," and asked me, "What does sin mean?" In the Greek it means to "miss the mark."

He then asked me, "What does a blueprint have on it?"

I said, "Markings or drawings."

Next He said, "Every person has missed their blueprint."

Because we've missed our blueprint, we've all "come short." This means we have not experienced the glory of God because we're inherently insufficient, lacking, and needy. We have missed God's personal opinion of us, which determines our infinite, intrinsic worth and value. We've missed our original identity, which can only come from God, who created us in His image and likeness.

As a result, life becomes all about getting our needs met. Anything on this list sound familiar?

- "I need to feel good about myself and my life."
- "I need to make a name for myself."
- "I need to be loved."
- "I need to look good."
- "I need to sound smart."
- "I need to feel like I measure up."
- "I need to be included."
- "I need my peers to like me."
- "I need to be good enough."
- "I need to be happy."
- "I need to be successful."
- "I need to feel valuable."
- "I need to be respected."
- "I need approval."

- "I need to be accepted."
- "I need attention."
- "I need to feel important."
- "I need to be heard."
- "I need to be cared about."
- "I need to be right."

In an attempt to meet these needs, some will work toward awards, promotions, and important titles to feel good about themselves. Others will buy expensive things to feel valuable. Even with all these things, eventually all you will feel are anxiety, anger, frustration, and depression.

Heart Tattoos

So many people are being defined and haunted by past experiences: what others have said to them, what they have said about them, and what they have done to them. We have a society that is filled with people who are suffering from physical, sexual, verbal, mental and social abuse. We hear stories every day related to violence, rape, sexual molestation, neglect, rejection, rage, dominance, name calling, put downs and bullying. As a result, they live feeling defective, degraded, disregarded, damaged, and depressed because their experiences have imprinted messages and images onto their hearts that define how they see and feel about themselves. I call these "Heart Tattoos."

Many have tried to deaden the pain by turning to drugs, alcohol, hobbies, relationships, and other things. Unfortunately, none of these things meet the real need, which keeps them going through the same cycles of life.

Several years ago I met a young lady in a recovery center who had been a prostitute. She showed me where her pimp had tattooed her, signifying that he "owned" her. Fortunately, the recovery center helped her erase these tattoos.

We can't erase the memory, but we can erase the message. God loves to heal the brokenhearted; deliver us from things that have trapped us in our past; and set us free from being bruised, crushed, and broken down in life. (Luke 4:18)

My heart tattoo was imprinted on me toward the end of my first-grade year. My teacher had called my mom and wanted to visit with her one afternoon after school. I went with her and sat outside the classroom while they visited. At the end of the meeting, I went into the classroom and they told me I needed to be held back in the first grade. At that moment, a message was sent into my heart that told me I was a failure.

As a result, I labeled myself as a "slow learner" and "stupid." I felt there was something wrong with me, that I didn't have the same abilities as other kids my age. I was able to convince my mom and my teacher to let me advance to the second grade, but the heart tattoo was already imprinted.

From that moment on, I hated school because it triggered these negative feelings about myself. I felt like I was going to a game I knew I was going to lose. I was convinced I couldn't make good grades.

In reality, I was offered a baseball scholarship upon graduating from high school. But I turned it down because I didn't want four more years of dealing with those tormenting feelings.

Since then, thankfully I have found my blueprint and allowed God to give me my identity and worth. When I imprinted this into my heart, it changed my life.

When you find your original blueprint, connect with the God who created it, and let the one who created you define you, all your needs get met. One of the greatest days of your life will be when you can say that you don't feel needy anymore.

Are you ready to connect with your blueprint and lose your neediness?

Chapter Three
Connecting With
Your Blueprint

I Thessalonians 5:23 gives us an understanding of who we are:

> "Now may the God of peace Himself sanctify you through and through [that is, separate you from profane and vulgar things, make you pure and whole and undamaged—consecrated to Him—set apart for His purpose]; and may <u>your spirit and soul and body</u> be kept complete and [be found] blameless at the coming of our Lord Jesus Christ." (Amplified, emphasis mine)

Our body, soul, and spirit collectively define our existence. Our physical body houses our soul and spirit and connects us to the material world: what we see, hear, taste, smell, and touch.

Our soul facilitates the mind, will, and emotions. It is the place where we think; reason; imagine; remember; make decisions; and experience emotions such as happiness, fear, anxiety, love, anger, and depression.

Our spirit facilitates our conscience, intuition, and communion. This is where we distinguish between right and wrong, where we experience our "gut feelings," and where God enables us to receive all the resources He needs to share with us and in us so we can have life and have it more abundantly.

Jesus gives us a better understanding of our spirit, soul, and body. He makes us aware that we are spiritual beings living in a physical body. He says in John 3:5, "Most assuredly, I say to you, unless one is born of water and the Spirit, he cannot enter the kingdom of God. That which is born of the flesh is flesh, and that which is born of the Spirit is spirit. Do not marvel that I said to you, you must be born again." (NKJV)

Jesus was explaining to Nicodemus that he was spiritually dead and separated from a life with God. His spirit needed to come to life so he could find his blueprint and be the original man God created him to be. Nicodemus could only see in the physical realm through the natural mind. He asks Jesus in John 3:4, How can a man be born when he is old? How do I enter back into my mother's womb a second time and be born? This didn't make any sense to him.

When we are spiritually dead, we don't have the ability to discern the things of God unless the Holy Spirit reveals them to us through God's Word. We don't have the ability to receive the resources God wants to provide to us and in us. That's why we all need to be born of the spirit.

The Divine Transplant

Ezekiel 36:26 says, "A new heart I will give you and a new spirit will I put within you, and I will take away the stony heart out of your flesh and give you a new heart of flesh."(AMP)

Suppose you take your son to the doctor for a checkup. After running the tests, the doctor gives you some bad news. Your child has a heart condition, and if left untreated, he will die. But then he says, "I have some good news. There is a transplant center that can find a heart for your child. They have patients who are willing to donate their heart after they pass away." Would you be interested? Of course, you would be.

Then one day you get a call from the transplant team telling you to bring your child to the hospital. They have a heart ready. The doctor takes your son into surgery where he removes the heart that is dying and puts in a new healthy heart. He comes out and tells you the good news, "Your son is going to live."

I have experienced firsthand the amazing impact a transplant can have on an individual's life. When my son was diagnosed with complete kidney failure, the doctors told us the only way he would live a long, healthy life would be to receive a new kidney from a donor. If he did not get a transplant, his body would continue to degrade, and his quality of life would continue to dwindle until he died.

Even with dialysis, he continued to struggle with feeling good. He often experienced fatigue, loss of appetite, swelling, and many other physical issues. But once he received his new kidney, he had energy, his appetite returned, and he was able to do all the things he enjoyed before he was sick. The transplant gave him new life!

This is exactly what happened when Jesus gave His life for us. Ephesians 2:1 says, "And you (He made alive), when you were dead (slain) by your trespasses and sins." (AMP) Ephesians 2:3 says, …"we were by nature children of wrath."

So the bad news is we were spiritually dead with no hope. But the Good News is that God so loved us that He gave His only Son (our spiritual donor) so we could have everlasting life. When we get born again, we get a new spirit that is alive and connected to God. This is what I call the "Divine Transplant."

Receiving the Transplant

John 14:6 says, "Jesus said to him, I am the Way, the Truth, and the Life: no one comes to the Father, except by (through) Me." (AMP)

Jesus is the only way to connect with the God who designed us, and Romans 10:9-10 tells us how to do that:

> "Because if you acknowledge and confess with your lips that Jesus is Lord and in your heart believe (adhere to, trust in and rely on the truth) that God raised Him from the dead, you will

be saved. For with the heart a person believes (adheres to, trust in and relies on Christ) and so is justified (declared righteous, acceptable to God), and with the mouth he confesses (declares openly and speaks freely his faith) and confirms (his) salvation." (AMP)

To receive the divine transplant and become born again, simply pray this prayer:

"Jesus, I believe you died on the cross for my sins, and I believe God raised You from the dead. I now confess with my mouth that Jesus is my Lord and Savior. Thank you for loving me, saving me from my sins, and accepting me as your child."

God is all about family. Daddy God now has another child birthed into His family.

John 1:12 says, "But as many as received him, to them gave he power to become the sons of God, even to them that believe on his name." (KJV)

There's a birthday party going on for you in heaven. Luke 15:10 says, "Likewise, I say to you, there is joy in the presence of the angels of God over one sinner that repents." (KJV)

Welcome to the family of God! Now it's time to build your infrastructure.

Chapter Four
Building Your Infrastructure

According to *Wikipedia*, an infrastructure is "the set of facilities and systems that serve a country, city, or other area, and encompasses the services and facilities necessary for its economy, households and firms to function." In other words, it provides the framework for a structure to develop.

Before a builder builds a house, he must clear the property, level it, build a road to it, install utilities and footing, and finally pour the foundation. Failing to do these things properly means the house will never function the way it was designed. If there are no electrical lines into the house, there won't be any light even if light switches are installed. If there is no water line, no water will come out of any faucet.

The infrastructure of our spiritual lives is laid in our inner man. In other words, we live out of our spirit and soul. If our infrastructure isn't laid properly, our lives will never function the way they were designed. This is why so many people live their lives frustrated.

Jesus says in Matthew 11:28-30:

"Are you tired? Worn out? Burned out on religion? Come to me. Get away with me and you'll recover your life. I'll show you how to take a real rest. Walk with me and work with me-Watch how I do it. Learn the unforced rhythms of grace. I won't lay anything heavy or ill-fitting on you. Keep company with me and you'll learn to live freely and lightly." (MSG)

He's saying, "I understand that you're struggling, worn down, stressed out, and tired of carrying the load. I want you to come with Me. You're going to walk with Me, work with Me, and watch how I do life. I'm going to show you how to operate in the unforced rhythms of grace. You're going to understand what it's like to live easy and light. It's like I'm going to help you lay all the utilities in your house, so when you hit the light switch or turn on the faucet, you will have lights and water."

I'm enjoying this lifestyle every day. When you hit what I call the WOW zone, where you're in the unforced rhythms of grace, then you begin to experience what Jesus meant about having life more abundantly. It means that your inner man is doing well despite outside circumstances.

To experience this kind of lifestyle you must implement some key foundational beliefs into your heart.

Your infrastructure has to be founded on Jesus and what He did for you through His death, burial, and resurrection. 1 Corinthians 3:11 says, "For no other foundation can anyone lay than that is laid, which is Jesus Christ." (KJV)

Ephesians 4:21 says, "If so be that you have heard him, and have been taught by him, as the truth is in Jesus." (KJV)

In order to get to know Jesus I always encourage people to read the four gospels: Matthew, Mark, Luke, and John. Watch what Jesus says and does. Watch how He treats people. When you see the true nature and character of Jesus, then you see the true nature and character of God.

Since we were created in His image and likeness, we begin to see what our new nature and character look like since we became born again. 2 Peter 1:4 says, "Whereby are given unto us exceeding great and precious promises; that by these you might be partakers of the divine nature, having escaped the corruption that is in the world through lust." (KJV) Since Jesus is the truth, when we become founded on what He accomplished for us, we are building on a solid foundation. John 8:32 tells us that when we know the truth, the truth will make us free.

The first thing we have to do is put off the old man. Ephesians 4:22-24 says:

> "That you put off concerning the former conversation the old man, which is corrupt according to the deceitful lust; And be renewed in the spirit of your mind; And that you put on the new man, which after God is created in righteousness and true holiness." (KJV)

Builders on TV shows that focus on home renovations usually start with a sledge hammer to tear out the kitchen, bathrooms, flooring, and sometimes walls to open up the inside of the house. Many times they take the home down to the shell. When we get born again, the first thing we should do is tear out old beliefs in our heart that came from what people said to us, about us, and did to us. We need to get rid of the old labels.

The next thing we have to do is renew the spirit of our mind. Romans 12:2 says, "And be not conformed to this world; but be ye transformed by the renewing of your mind, that you may prove what is that good, and acceptable, and perfect, will of God." (KJV) Renewing the mind is more than just changing the thoughts in our natural mind. It is about changing the thoughts in our heart. This is the real definition of repentance. It is where we exchange the old beliefs in our heart with new heart beliefs that come from God's Word.

If we are going to see a real transformation, we must get into the spiritual mind of our heart, not just have it in the intellectual mind in our head. The spiritual heart is where our beliefs, convictions, judgments, opinions, and viewpoints are stored.

How you see and feel about yourself, life, other people, and God are coming out of your heart at this very moment.

Several years ago, I asked the Lord why so many Christians are struggling in their lives. He told me. "They've never gone through the process of renewing the spirit of their minds. They aren't really seeing themselves the way I see them. Listen to what they are saying about themselves."

Immediately I heard the words, "I'm just a sinner saved by grace." These individuals know they have been forgiven of their sins and they are saved, but they still see themselves as the old man, leaving them with feelings of insecurity, inferiority, and insufficiency.

Many people also say, "God knows I'm not perfect." These individuals have that gnawing feeling that God is rarely pleased with them. This is an example of trying to live a new life in Christ with the "old man insufficient sinner" mentality.

For many years I served as the founder and executive director of two recovery centers. I love helping people who are having life-controlling problems. I totally understand why addicts need to admit they are addicts and need help, but when they label themselves as "once an alcoholic, always an alcoholic," they will see themselves as a sober addict for the rest of their lives. I'm very happy they are sober, but they live with that gnawing feeling of being defective and flawed. They live in recovery but are never recovered.

My goal is that we are all set free from any belief about ourselves that doesn't match our blueprint. Proverbs 23:7 says, "For as he thinks in his heart so is he." (KJV) Whatever we believe about ourselves in our heart has created our state of being. The state of our being creates our behaviors. Our behaviors are manifesting the fruit in our lives.

This is why God tells us to put on the new man. 2 Corinthians 5:17 says, "Therefore, if anyone is in Christ, he is a new creation; old things have passed away; behold, all things have become new." (KJV) New means the original. The original is the person God saw before you were born.

2 Corinthians 5:21 says, "For he hath made him to be sin for us, who knew no sin; that we might be made the righteousness of God in him." (KJV) This is the you that God created in righteousness and true holiness. Righteousness means divine approval.

Even though we still sin sometimes, we are legally and positionally in a right standing with God because of what Jesus did for us. I know many people wonder about what to do when they sin. I'll give you an analogy, I'm a clean person because I shower every morning. But as I go through my day I can get dirty. Sometimes I spill things on myself, other people get something on me or stuff blowing in the air will get on me. I'm still a clean person but got dirty. All I do is take a shower or wash it off. Every morning I take a spiritual shower during my prayer time to get the junk from the world or something

I"ve said or done that didn't reflect His nature and character off my soul and heart. I wash in the water of the Word. I say, "Lord, I thank you for cleansing my heart and soul from anything that isn't like You"

I know when God pulls up my spiritual x-ray to see my spiritual man, He sees that new man. He sees that righteous man that's created in Christ Jesus. When I look into the mirror of the Word, I see the same thing God is seeing.

The Apostle Paul was born Saul (the old man). Saul was a man who was ordering believers to be killed. He was living his life the way he believed he should. All the while Saul is persecuting the church, God had already drawn up a blueprint for Paul. Saul had never seen it until the day God turned the light on in Acts 9 so Saul could see Paul's blueprint. At that moment, Saul called out to the Lord and became Paul, the new man created in Christ Jesus. From that point on, Paul started seeing himself the way God was seeing him and began to live the life God created for him so he could start fulfilling his purpose.

Psalm 1:2-3 tells us what this looks like:

> "But his delight and desire are in the law of the Lord, on His law (the precepts, instructions, and

teaching of God) he habitually meditates (ponders and studies) by day and by night. And he shall be like a tree firmly planted (and tended) by the streams of water, ready to bring forth its fruit in its season; its leaf shall not fade or wither; and everything he does shall prosper (and come to maturity)" (AMP).

When we put off all those negative, destructive, lying beliefs about ourselves; let God tell us who we are; and put on the new, true beliefs that define how God sees us, then we'll start bearing fruit that comes from his nature and character.

Here is something I want you to do. This is what the Bible calls meditating on the Word of God. When you got your Divine Transplant (Ezekiel 36:26-27), he took away your stony heart and replaced it with a new heart and a new spirit. Ask the Holy Spirit to help you see God taking out the stony heart and putting in your new heart. You went through spiritual surgery. The exchange has been made and you are a new creation. See yourself (get a picture in your mind and heart) as a new person. Think on it until it gets implemented into your heart. This is one way of bringing your thoughts into the obedience of Christ.

Before I go to sleep or first thing in the morning, I meditate on the things God is saying about me. So then faith comes by hearing, and hearing by the Word of God. (Romans 10:17)

One day I was talking to a minister about seeing myself the way God sees me. He told me God had chosen him. I said "Absolutely." Then I asked him, "What do you look like chosen?" He gave me a definition of chosen. This is where so many of us live. Intellectually we can tell someone what chosen means, but we can get stumped when we are asked to make it personal.

I went home that night and asked the Holy Spirit to reveal to me what I look like chosen. All of a sudden, a video went through my mind.

I was in an open field with thousands of other people standing together, side by side. Then we saw a man walking in the distance. As he got closer, we recognized him as Jesus. He came close to the crowd and stopped. I was back deep in the crowd, but when He stopped, He looked at me, pointed his finger directly at me, and said, "Gary, come here." Out of thousands of people, He saw me and picked me out. It made me feel so special and I realized how He sees us as individuals.

He is no respecter of persons. It wasn't that the rest of the crowd wasn't chosen, but since I had asked, I received.

For the rest of my life, I will have this picture in my mind. Such a powerful feeling comes over me every time I revisit that picture.

When I pray, I go through pictures God has given me. I call it God's photo album. This has taken my faith to a new level.

I want the same for all of you! God loves you and He wants you to see yourself exactly the way He sees you, right now!

Chapter Five
What You Are Worth

If you want to find out what something is worth, you look at the purchase price, not the appraisal. It is the amount of money that someone will actually pay for an item that determines its worth. If your car, for example, appraises for $30,000, and someone offers to buy it for $40,000, then it's worth $40,000 to the person who bought it, even if no one else thinks it's worth that much.

Where is your worth coming from? From what other people think you're worth? People usually appraise our value by what we have, what we know, or what we have done. Our worth can also come from our own appraisal of those things.

If the appraisal is the framework supporting your worth, you will face an enormous amount of pressure in your life because you'll always look to something or someone to confirm your worth. This doesn't work and never will because we are not created to provide the framework that is supporting our worth. Over time, mental, emotional, and physical issues will start showing themselves, leading to family, work, social, or financial problems. Most individuals try to fix the problem rather than addressing the framework issue.

The solution is to discover our true worth based on our purchase price. 1 Corinthians 6:20 says, "You were bought with a price (purchased with a preciousness and paid for, made His own). So then, honor and bring glory to him in your body." (AMP) Our purchase price was the life of Jesus founded on His love for us. John 3:16 says, "For God so loved the world (You) that He gave His only begotten Son, that whoever (You) believeth in Him should not perish, but have everlasting life." (KJV)

John 15:13 says, "Greater love has no one than this, than to lay down one's life for his friends." (KJV) Going back to the Divine Transplant, you have just been diagnosed with heart disease. The doctor tells you that unless you get a heart transplant, you are going to die. About that time a man walks in and says, "I have a perfectly healthy heart and I want to give it to you."

But you say, "You'll die if you give me your heart."

He replies, "You are worth it. Your life is very important, and I don't want you to die. There is a reason you are on this earth, and you have some things that need to be done. Not only that, but if you get my heart, you will live forever."

This is what the love of God looks like. God said, "I have a Son who is willing to die for you so you can have a new life." Jesus is the only one who has the perfect blood type and can give you a healthy heart that enables you to live forever. This is what the birth, life, death, burial, and resurrection of Jesus is all about.

You had no hope, and you were spiritually dying, but God saw tremendous value in you. In the heart of God, you were worth so much that He purchased you with the life of His Son. For God so loved you!

Read Matthew 27 and 28 to grasp the depth of God's love for you. Watch a play or movie that depicts these scenes (the "Passion of the Christ," for example) to help you get the picture. As you are reading or watching what Jesus is going through, see yourself in the story. You are standing in the crowd as the people are yelling, "Crucify Him!" Then see yourself watching as they scourge Him.

As Jesus is being taken to Golgotha to be crucified, imagine yourself standing there as they are nailing Him to the cross. Now, while He is hanging on the cross with the crown of thorns on His head and blood flowing off His body, see yourself as the only person at His feet. Look up into His eyes, see and hear Jesus call you by your name, and say these words: "I love you."

I like to put on some soft instrumental worship music. Then I close my eyes and picture Jesus looking and talking to me while He was dying on the cross.

Three important things you will experience as you are meditating on God's word: 1) His attention, 2) His affection, and 3) His affirmation. Every morning before you start your day, repeat this process. After a while, this picture will be ingrained into your mind and heart, and you will be able to trigger it anytime, day or night. Then you will find yourself experiencing the love of God.

When we experience the love of God daily, Romans 5:5 says, "And hope maketh not ashamed; because the love of God has been shed abroad in our hearts by the Holy Ghost which is given unto us." (KJV)

On October 11, 2011, in the middle of the night, I had an encounter with the love of God that transformed my life. For several hours He demonstrated to me the power of not just knowing He loved me, but actually experiencing His love. He began to explain that His love was setting the atmosphere and environment in my heart for faith to work.

He took me to Genesis 1:2: "And the earth was without form, and void; and darkness was upon the face of the deep. And the Spirit of God moved upon the face of the waters." (KJV) The word "moved" translates as *hovering* or *brooding*. He explained that since God is love, and the Holy Spirit is the third person of the Godhead, before He ever said, "Let there be," the Holy Spirit had to set the atmosphere and environment with the love of God.

Galatians 5:6 says, "For in Jesus Christ neither circumcision availeth any thing, nor uncircumcision, but faith which worketh by love." (KJV) Everything in the Kingdom of God only works by love.

After I encountered His atmosphere of love, my heart was so much more open to hearing and receiving from the Holy Spirit. Now, when I study the Bible, the words jump off the page more than ever. I am getting a better understanding of what He is showing me. My faith has begun to grow more quickly.

In this atmosphere of feeling safe and secure, there is no rejection. This truth enabled me to open up to His correction and discipline. I don't see correction as rejection; I see that my Father cares about me. I love when He shows me I am missing something or going in the wrong direction.

It is like a father telling his child to get out of the street before he gets run over. It is vital that you see God as a loving Father (Daddy God) who has a consuming passion for your well-being. Think about how much you love your child. Your Heavenly Father loves you more than you love your child.

He also explained to me that in His loving atmosphere, His perfect love casts out all fear. 1 John 4:18 says, "There is no fear in love; but perfect love casteth out fear: because fear has torment. He that feareth is not made perfect in love." (KJV)

If your home has an air conditioner, but it is not turned on and it is 90 degrees inside your house, you can turn the unit on and set the thermostat to 72 degrees. The cold air will start removing the hot air, bringing the temperature to the 72-degree mark. No matter how hot it is outside, you are comfortable inside.

As we are experiencing the love of God, it takes over our hearts and casts out all our feelings of insecurity, inferiority, and insufficiency. Once we start focusing on the solution, the problem starts going away.

A couple of years ago my wife and I decided to go on the Weight Watchers eating plan. She sat me down and explained that I would get a certain number of points per day. Before I put anything in my mouth, I needed to add up the points to see how many I would be using.

Something clicked in my mind. I told her that rather than focusing on losing weight, I would focus solely on my points. I believed that if I kept to the plan, the weight would naturally come off. Sure enough, I began to lose weight. As I continued this process, eventually I reached my goal.

We make things harder than they need to be. If we will focus on getting our heart in line with God's plan, we will start experiencing His "easy and light."

The Lord took me to Ephesians 3:17: "That Christ may dwell in your hearts by faith; that you, being rooted and grounded in love." (KJV) Every morning before I start my day, I trigger the love of God in my heart. I see myself walking along a beach and looking at the ocean. The sound of the waves, the sunny sky, and the dawning of a new day comprise the peaceful atmosphere.

As I am walking, I see a man approaching. As He gets closer, I see the Lord Jesus. At this point I am in awe of His presence. I see Him look me in the eyes, giving me His *attention*.

Then I see Him reach His arms out to give me a hug, which shows me *affection*. As we embrace, I hear Him say, "Good morning, Gary, I love you." Here He is giving me *affirmation*.

I then say to Him, "Jesus, I love you and I want to thank you for all you've done for me." Many times I just start naming some of those things.

One morning, as I told Him I loved Him, He told me, "I loved you first."

I smiled and said, "Yes, you did." At that moment I felt the depth of His love for me.

Every day as I am experiencing His love, it keeps confirming how valuable I am to Him. I start each day knowing that God respects me. By the time I walk out the door, I don't need anyone to give me attention, affirmation, or affection because those needs are already met. I am good to go!

Chapter Six
What You Have

Let's use a computer to illustrate "what we have." When you purchase a computer, it comes in all different shapes, sizes, and colors with certain features already installed. When you click on the software apps, you will discover what is already available for you. You may find a program called "Word," which will give you access to templates that can help you build a resume, type a report, create a brochure, make a calendar, or design a flyer.

Even though there are multiple programs installed, you are limited to those available in this machine. Then you get an internet connection, which connects your computer to a worldwide system of networks. Suddenly, you are no longer limited to what is installed on your computer. You now have access to resources, information, and communication from other networks from all over the world. You can send emails, connect to social media, shop from home, manage bank accounts, watch television, listen to music, or watch videos online. There are almost no limits to what you can do through the internet.

Before we were born again, we were like the computer that had been installed with certain gifts, talent, and abilities. We used what was already installed to live life. We began utilizing the abilities of our body to see, feel, touch, hear, and taste. We use our soul (mind, will, and emotions) in many different ways. We started going to school to get an education. We began making decisions about what we wanted to do or where we wanted to go.

Soon we began expressing the gifts God had installed into our lives. Some of us began to play instruments, sing songs, draw pictures, build things, or play sports. Unfortunately, we didn't receive every gift and ability, which limited what we could do. As we learned in "Missing The Mark," we were born insufficient.

When we got born again, we got connected to the Heavenly Internet through the person of the Holy Spirit. 1 Corinthians 3:16 says, "Know ye not that ye are the temple of God and that the Spirit of God dwelleth in You?" (KJV) 1 Corinthians 6:19 says, "What? Know ye not that your body is the temple of the Holy Ghost who is in you, which ye have of God, and ye are not your own?" (KJV)

When the Holy Spirit came to live inside us, our potential was upgraded from "limited" to "unlimited." That changes everything. We can never exhaust all the works of the Holy Spirit, but we can lay a solid foundation of seeing Him working in our lives. We need to ask ourselves three questions:

1. What does the Holy Spirit have?
2. What does the Holy Spirit know?
3. What does the Holy Spirit do?

What Does The Holy Spirit Have?

Romans 8:11 says, "But if the Spirit of him that raised Jesus from the dead dwell in you, he that raised up Christ from the dead shall also quicken your mortal bodies by his Spirit that dwelleth in you." (KJV)

If the Holy Spirit raised Jesus from the dead and He lives in you, how much power do you have in your life? One day I was trying to grasp the reality of how much power I had. The Holy Spirit gave me an example of a man needing to clear out acres of trees. He was using an ax to chop the trees when another man drove up with a bulldozer.

Clearing acres of trees with an ax will take a long time. Plus, stumps would be left everywhere, so the land wouldn't really be clear. The bulldozer, on the other hand, would do the work for you much faster. Plus, the trees would be uprooted, not just cut down, so the land is cleared and ready to use.

In Hebrews 10:29, the Holy Spirit is called the Spirit of grace. Grace is God's ability deposited into your life, enabling you to do what you cannot do yourself. Romans 6:14 says, "For sin shall not have dominion over you, for ye are not under law, but under grace." (KJV) When we were dead in our trespasses and sins, He made us alive. Romans 8:2 says, "For the law of the Spirit of life in Christ Jesus hath made me free from the law of sin and death." (KJV)

The Holy Spirit enables us to live an overcoming life by His power, not ours. I am no longer using that ax to try to live a victorious life. I am now climbing on the bulldozer that has the power I need to live. Ask the Holy Spirit to reveal this Truth into your heart. Take a moment each morning to see yourself with unlimited power. The picture of the ax and bulldozer stirs up that gift of grace inside me. It triggers my heart, mind, and feelings with incredible strength.

What Does The Holy Spirit Know?

John 14:16-17 says: "And I will pray the Father, and He will give you another Helper, that He may abide with you forever—the Spirit of truth, whom the world cannot receive, because it neither sees Him nor knows Him; but you know Him, for He dwells with you and will be in you." (NKJV)

John 14:26 says: "But the Helper, the Holy Spirit, whom the Father will send in My name, He will teach you all things, and bring to your remembrance all things that I said to you." (NKJV)

John 16:13 says: "However, when He, the Spirit of truth, has come, He will guide you into all truth; for He will not speak on His own authority, but whatever He hears He will speak; and He will tell you things to come." (NKJV)

The Holy Spirit knows the Truth and His sword is the Word of God! Ephesians 6:17 says,

"And take the helmet of salvation, and the sword of the Spirit, which is the word of God;" (KJV) The Word of God is the instrument through which the Holy Spirit works.

John 6:63 says, "It is the Spirit who gives life; (He is the Life-giver);the flesh conveys no benefit whatsoever (there is no profit in it). The words (truth) that I have been speaking to you are spirit and life." (AMP) John 17:17 says, "Sanctify them through thy truth. thy word is truth." (KJV) This is such a powerful combination when we have the Word of God and the Holy Spirit living in us. In a world that is full of lies and deception, as John 8:32 says, we can know the Truth and the Truth shall make us free.

I have heard so many things come from the outside world that I knew weren't the Truth. Those who do not have the Spirit of Truth are easily led by what they see, hear, and feel is true. Proverbs 14:12 says, "There is a way which seems right to a man and appears straight before him, but at the end of it is the way of death." (AMP)

The Holy Spirit knows the things God has prepared for us to do. 1 Corinthians 2:9-12 says:

"But as it is written: Eye has not seen, not ear heard, Nor have entered into the heart of man the things which God has prepared for those who love Him. But God has revealed them to us through His Spirit. For the Spirit searches all things, yes, the deep things of God. For what man knows the things of a man except the Spirit of God. Now we have received, not the spirit of the world, but the Spirit who is from God, that we might know the things that have been freely given to us by God." (NKJV)

As God is building your life according to His blueprint, every day the Holy Spirit knows what God has prepared for your life. But we have to acknowledge Him and expect Him to reveal those things to us. God may make divine appointments for us, assign people to cross our path, give us nuggets of wisdom and understanding, or present opportunities to us.

If you get up in the morning anticipating these kinds of things to happen in your life, everyday will feel like Christmas. You'll always start the day wondering what God has for you!

What Does The Holy Spirit Do?

The Holy Spirit does so many things, but one thing He does that totally transforms our lives is that He produces fruit! Galatians 5:22-23 says, "But the fruit of the Spirit is love, peace, longsuffering, gentleness, goodness, faith, meekness, temperance: against such there is no law." (KJV)

When the Holy Spirit moves into us, He brings His fruit with Him. This fruit is the manifestation of God's nature and character. Human effort cannot produce the fruit of the Spirit. These fruit can only come by the work that His presence accomplishes within us. According to *MacLaren's Expositions*, "The individual members (fruit) are isolated graces, but all connected, springing from one root and constituting an organic whole."

Many Christians say, "I need to pray for more patience" when they are already loaded with patience. Patience does not come from what we can do; it comes from what the Holy Spirit has already deposited into your life.

Suppose a billionaire told you that if you opened a savings account, he would make a deposit into your account every day, and that would be enough for you to live on. You open the account but never transfer this money from your savings into your checking account. You have all the money you need, but you don't use it. This is how so many Christians live their lives. The Holy Spirit is putting His unlimited resources into their accounts, but they don't use these resources.

Let's see what the Holy Spirit has put into your account:

1. Love. *MacLaren's Expositions* says, "Love heads the list, as the foundation and moving principle of the rest. It is the life sap which rises through the tree and given form to all the clusters." As we are experiencing His consuming passion for our well-being (His attention, affection, affirmation, actions, and discipline). Love creates the atmosphere for all other fruit to manifest.

2. Joy. In His atmosphere of love, we are experiencing His grace and favor toward us. This creates feelings of great delight, pleasure, and satisfaction. The joy of the Lord is our strength.

3. Peace. Knowing we are in harmony with God creates our tranquil state of being where we experience security, safety, quietness, and rest. We are enjoying the sense of being whole and complete.

4. Longsuffering. This means being divinely regulated with endurance, constancy, steadfastness, and perseverance. It is the ability to endure something that incites, instigates, angers, or irritates. When misfortune, delay, hardship, or pain come, the Holy Spirit gives us the strength to endure.

5. Gentleness. This is the Spirit-produced uprightness, which avoids human harshness or cruelty. It means having the disposition working in us to hurt no one but to do all the good we can to everyone.

6. Goodness. This means being good-natured, conformed to what is moral and ethical, satisfactory in quality, well-behaved, friendly, honorable, genuine, sound, reliable, and pleasant.

7. Faithfulness. This is being trustworthy, dependable, loyal, and honest with our words, promises, and actions. It means being that person God and others can count on.

8. Meekness. This means being divinely balanced, calm, temperate, able to display the right blend of force and reserve when under provocation.

9. Temperance. This means being in control of ourselves. It is the divine ability empowering us to rule, control, master, and dominate our heart, soul, and body. It is a dominion that proceeds from within ourselves but not by ourselves.

When the line is long at the store, remind yourself, "I am loaded with patience." Every time I say that to myself, I immediately feel the presence of that grace settling me down. Sometimes the Holy Spirit will tell me, "Just relax and enjoy the moment." He never tells us to do something He hasn't empowered us to do. This is our new potential and our new way of living!

Now, meditate on the Word of God. Ask the Holy Spirit to help you see yourself loaded with all nine fruit. How do these graces work in your life every day? What do you look like being a patient person? A faithful person? A peaceful person? A loving person?

When you begin to see yourself loaded with these characteristics, you will be strong in the Lord and in the power of His might. If you process this, you will mature at an accelerated rate and be amazed at how fruitful your life is becoming.

Chapter Seven
Why You Are Here

When I ask people why they are on earth, many get the "deer in the headlights" look on their face. Some say, "I don't know, but I wish I did." Most people begin thinking in terms of being a doctor, lawyer, teacher, CEO, nurse, minister, missionary, coach, musician, artist, builder, inventor, entrepreneur, etc. While you may join one of these professions or callings at some point in your life, no matter how successful you become, if you miss your purpose, you will always feel empty.

Why Are You Here?

John 15:8 says you were created to bear fruit: "My Father is glorified and honored by this, when you bear much fruit, and prove yourselves to be My [true] disciples." (AMP) So, the purpose of your life is to be fruitful.

Suppose someone gives you an apple seed. First, you need to find some good ground to plant the seed in. Next, you need to prepare the soil with quality nutrients and plant the seed at the proper depth. Then you need to water and maintain the soil while the seed is growing. Eventually, this apple seed will begin to mature and you will discover an apple tree is starting to grow.

As it continues to grow, you will see apples growing on this tree. From these apples you can get more seeds to plant in the ground to produce more trees. Eventually you will develop an entire orchard. This is being fruitful. Out of this orchard you now have the ability to provide nourishment for other people.

Apples can be used to make applesauce, apple butter, apple pie, apple muffins, apple cake, or a caramel apple. Think about all the things you just produced from one seed and all the people it just fed. It didn't happen overnight, but as the seed continued to develop, grow, and mature, it eventually bore a fruitful harvest.

This is what God had in mind when He created you. God planted the seed of His nature and character in you at your new birth in Christ. As you have been building the infrastructure of life in the previous chapters, you have been watering the seed.

Every time you act on the Word of God, you are growing. As you have grown, you realize the Holy Spirit is producing all of His fruit in you. Since you have this fruit, you are able to start being fruitful.

Some people believe it takes years to be fruitful, but God's ability working in your life is supernatural. You can start being fruitful right now and fulfilling your purpose. Just as the one apple seed affected so many people, your seed of life is going to make an incredible impact on this world.

Are You Ready to Fulfill Your Purpose?

To discover your purpose, you must start in two places. Once you become fruitful in these places, you'll discover what you are on earth to do.

The first place you must start bearing fruit is in Matthew 22:37-38, "Jesus said unto him, Thou shalt love the Lord thy God with all thy heart, and with all thy soul, and with all thy mind. This is the first and great commandment." (KJV)

I start each day with a cup of coffee. Then I go into my office and pray using the Lord's prayer (Matthew 6:9-13) as my model. This means that I give Daddy God my attention, affection, and praise every morning. I thank Him for being my Heavenly Father and allowing me the privilege of being His son. I tell Him how much I love Him and appreciate everything He has done and is doing in my life. This triggers in my heart and mind all He is doing for me and sets my day in motion for giving Him respect and honor and affirming our Father-son relationship.

Then I give the Lord Jesus my attention, affection, and praise. As I shared earlier, I see myself embracing Him, telling Him how much I love Him, and thanking Him for giving His life for me. This is always a special moment of my morning. It triggers how much He loves me, and I feel His presence with me all day. I can feel His strength rising up inside me.

Then I give the Holy Spirit my attention, thanking him for all he is doing in my life. This triggers in my heart and mind that he is my helper, strengthener, and counselor.

After I have been in communion with my Heavenly Father, my heart is open, trusting, and receptive to hearing from Him. So, I open my Bible and read the scriptures to receive His direction, encouragement, and correction. As you spend time in fellowship with Him and hearing Him speak to you through His Word, your beliefs, appetites, affections, attitudes, and actions are all going to start conforming to His will, and you will naturally want to obey him.

John 15:9-11 says:

"I have loved you just as the Father has loved Me; remain in My love [and do not doubt My love for you]. If you keep My commandments and obey My teaching, you will remain in My love, just as I have kept My Father's commandments and remain in His love. I have told you these things so that My joy and delight may be in you, and that your joy may be made full and complete and overflowing." (AMP)

Inside this love zone you will experience so much joy. Remember, you always express what you are experiencing.

Because you are loving the Lord, you will find your second purpose in life. Matthew 22:39 says, "And the second is like unto it, you shall love your neighbor as yourself." (KJV) Our first neighbors are our family members.

Husbands and Wives

Husbands, when you experience the love of the Heavenly Father, you will be compelled to love your wives as Christ loves the church. Wives, when you are experiencing God's love in your heart, this stream of love will compel you to love your husband.

Love never fails! When love is flowing in a relationship, divorce will never be in the future. Here are some practical ways to give your spouse attention, affection, and affirmation to keep your marriage rock-solid:

1. Attention: "Honey, how was your day? Anything interesting happen?" Now put your cell phone down for a little bit and look your spouse in the eye when he or she is answering your questions.

If you're the one answering, don't just say, "Fine," or "It stunk." Give your spouse a little detail to pinpoint something that stood out. Love cares about what is going on in the other person's life.

2. Affection: "Honey, I want you to know how much I really love and appreciate you." Give hugs and kisses. Hold hands and cuddle with each other. This keeps the bond tight.

3. Affirmation: "Honey, you are such a good wife/husband to me and I really appreciate you." Show support by giving approval and encouragement. Compliment your spouse on the way he or she looks or something he or she has done.

4. Action: Do special things for each other and with each other. "How about going on a date with me Saturday night? We can leave the kids with a babysitter." Make it a night of romance and passion. Have fun together at least once a month. Marriage can either be Heaven or Hell on earth. When love is working in the marriage, Heaven is in the home.

Parents

If you are a parent, God has drawn a blueprint for your child. Your purpose is to nurture and train your child according to his or her blueprint. Regardless of whether your parents were good role models, your Heavenly Father, the greatest role model ever, has a blueprint for parenting. But you must set the atmosphere first, which starts with having a loving relationship with your Heavenly Father. Then let His love flow out of you to create a loving atmosphere in your home. In order for your children to grow up healthy, they must be living in an atmosphere of God's love.

As your Heavenly Father is giving you His attention, affection, affirmation, action, and correction, you will be giving those to your children. Here is what this looks like in practical application:

1. Give your children attention. Ask them, "How are things going at school or with your friends? Anything exciting going on? How did your day go?" After you ask a question, give them time to answer. You want them to know you are interested in their lives. During the dialogue, you will be able to hear what is going on in their hearts.

2. Give them affection. They need to experience a loving touch, a hug, a kiss, or a pat on the back.

3. Give them affirmation. Find something positive to say to or about your children every day. Compliment them on something they did, how they look, etc. Children excel in a complimentary atmosphere.

4. Give your children action. They need their parents to be involved in their lives. Putting food on the table and a roof over their heads is not enough. They need their parents to go places with them, do things with them, and attend their events.

5. Give them correction. When you have set an atmosphere of love by doing the first four love characteristics, correction will be a positive. When God is correcting or disciplining us, He is pruning. He is removing the dead, non-productive things (attitudes, affections, appetites, and actions) in our lives. After we have been pruned, we are healthier which makes room for new growth and more fruitfulness. This is the purpose for correcting your children.

One day your children will look back and thank you for what you did and how you did it, even though it hurt at the time.

Other Family Relationships

How are you giving your parents, grandparents, and siblings attention, affection, affirmation, and acts of kindness? Each family member needs to ask himself or herself this question and then start fulfilling that purpose.

Over the years I have watched so many ministers and businessmen and women neglect their families, building a church, career, or business. I once heard a story of a preacher's daughter who was attending her father's funeral. She made the statement, "He was a good man. I just wish I would have known him." God's blueprint is always in order. Love God first, then family, and finally your other neighbors.

Your Neighbors

These are the individuals we come in contact with during our day. What would our world look like if every morning we loved our neighbors by giving them attention, affection, affirmation, and action that lines up with the fruit of the Spirit? 1 Corinthians 13:4-8 is the blueprint for what loves looks like in action:

"Love endured with patience and serenity, love is kind and thoughtful, and is not jealous or envious; love does not brag and is not proud or arrogant. It is not rude, it is not self-seeking, it is not provoked [nor overly sensitive and easily angered]; it does not take in to account a wrong endured. It does not rejoice at injustice, but rejoices with the truth [when right and truth prevail]. Love bears all things [regardless of what comes], believes all things [looking for the best in each one], hopes all things [remaining steadfast during difficult times], endures all things [without weakening]. Love never fails [it never fades nor ends]. But as for prophecies, they will pass away; as for tongues, they will cease; as for the gift of special knowledge, it will pass away." (AMP)

Love causes us to demonstrate the other eight fruit of the Spirit. The world needs to see the nature and character of God in action. People in the world are not responding to theology; they are responding and repenting when they see the goodness of God. (Romans 2:4)

Before you walk out the door in the morning, visualize your purpose, which is to love people. Before you get to work, see yourself loving your boss and work associates. Walk in the room and give them a "Hello, how are you today?" with a smile and a complimentary word.

During the day, demonstrate all nine fruit of the Spirit. Rather than gossiping or complaining about other people, show acts of kindness, be patient, encourage them, find the good they are doing, and brag on them. God wants you to use your workplace to fulfill your purpose. There should be more ministry going on outside the church than inside the church.

When you walk into a restaurant, let the waiter or waitress experience what God's love looks and feels like. Greet them with a smiling face. As they are serving you, let them hear "Thank you." Look for ways to compliment them. If they forget to bring you something or the meal is taking longer than expected, just draw on the fruit of kindness and patience, which the Holy Spirit has already loaded you with. Lastly, leave them a big tip.

If you leave the love of God everywhere you go, others will taste and see that the Lord is good and want to know our loving Heavenly Father, as well.

Matthew 28:19-20 illustrates the greatest way to love our neighbors:

> "Go therefore and make disciples of all the nations [help the people to learn of Me, believe in Me, and obey My words], baptizing them in the name of the Father and of the Son and of the Holy Spirit, teaching them to observe everything that I have commanded you; and lo, I am with you always [remaining with you perpetually-regardless of circumstances, and on every occasion], even to the end of the age." (AMP)

Whether God has called you into the five-fold ministry (Ephesians 4) or whether you are a doctor, lawyer, teacher, plumber, nurse, musician, artist, builder, inventor, or entrepreneur, your ultimate purpose is to lead people into a loving relationship with the Heavenly Father and help them find their blueprint so they can fulfill their purpose.

Use the first three chapters of this book as a template. Tell them you have been reading a book called *Finding Your Blueprint*. Ask them, "Did you know that before you were born, God knew you and had drawn a blueprint for your life?" Then tell them that God defined five things in their blueprint: 1) what they are, 2) who they are, 3) what they are worth, 4) what they have, and 5) why they are here.

If they seem drawn into what you are sharing, then follow chapters two and three to show them how to find their blueprint. Use the prayer in chapter three to lead them to the Lord and connect them to the God who created their blueprint. Get them a copy of the book so they can begin building their infrastructure and being fruitful.

Now you'll begin seeing how many your life is affecting from the seed God planted in you! You sowed a seed from your life. Now they can take the seed God has given them and sow it into others. This is where we see the harvest coming together. The love of God will change the world.

There isn't anything greater than having a loving relationship with the Heavenly Father, following your blueprint, bearing fruit, and fulfilling your purpose. Then when your life is over, you will hear, "Well done thou good and faithful servant."

Closing Thoughts

Any time God is trying to teach me something, He tells me to stay on this subject until I get it into my heart. It's going to be vitally important for you to continue to build your infrastructure. Seeing and feeling about yourself the same way God is seeing and feeling about you. Learning how to live your life from His perspective of you. In the morning, revisit God's photos He has shown you about the Divine transplant, being a new creation, righteous, loved by your Daddy God, having the person of the Holy Spirit working in you and fulfilling your purpose. After doing this for a while, you'll find it happening more naturally. It only takes me a couple minutes to trigger these thoughts now and many times I find my mind during the day going back to them. What's so powerful is I can experience God's love and presence all day long.

Remember whatever you are experiencing will be what you will be expressing each day.

I'm going to be offering more advanced teaching and coaching on building your blueprint. If you are interested, you can reach me at: www.findingyourblueprint.org.